modern
mantras

www.youaretheauthor.com

modern mantras

www.youaretheauthor.com

First edition for the United States, its territories
and dependencies, and Canada published 2002
by Barron's Educational Series, Inc.

Conceived and created by
Axis Publishing Limited
8c Accommodation Road
London NW11 8ED
www.axispublishing.co.uk

Creative Director: Siân Keogh
Project Designer: Juliet Brown
Managing Editor: Matthew Harvey
Project Editor: Michael Spilling
Production Manager: Sue Bayliss

All inquiries should be addressed to:
Barron's Educational Series, Inc.
250 Wireless Boulevard
Hauppauge, New York 11788
http://www.barronseduc.com

Library of Congress Catalog Card No:
2001094353

ISBN 0-7641-5523-7

9 8 7 6 5 4 3 2 1

Separation by United Graphic Pte Limited
Printed and bound in China by Toppan Printing

contents

what is a mantra?

Mantras originate from the specialist branches of the Hindu and Buddhist religions that involve the ritual repetition of sacred phrases and texts. A mantra is a syllable, word, or phrase that can be repeated in a chant-like fashion, either out loud or silently in your thoughts. The most famous of these powerful mantras has just six syllables:

"Om mani padme hum"

Untranslatable into English, the sounds of this ancient mantra are said to contain the central mysteries of Buddhist teaching. Buddhist monks spend many hours of their day repeating this and other mantras. The practice helps them to clear their minds of distracting thought and sounds during meditation and, over many years, can bring them closer to attaining enlightenment.

the power of mantras

Mantras are traditionally believed to possess great spiritual power. Today, many people harness the power of the mantra to make sense of the world, their experiences, and their relationships, and by doing so improve the quality of their lives. A mantra can distil in a few words an important truth that helps keep your life balanced and healthy instead of following negative, instinctive behaviors.

All modern mantras contain some essential truth or lesson about ourselves or the world we live in. They have a special meaning to the individual using them. You've probably been using modern mantras for years without realizing it. Just the simple phrase, "Keep calm," is a great example—it can help you to remain focused in a stressful or difficult situation and to remember your objectives.

www.youaret

This book is a collection of phrases carefully selected from the hundreds of contributions sent to our website, *www.youaretheauthor.com*. These modern mantras are mostly a couple of sentences, a phrase, or even just a word that people use to get them through whatever life throws at them. Some of the mantras will make you laugh, some will make you angry, while others, we hope, will make you

eauthor.com

nod in agreement; all of them contain some nugget of human wisdom that will inspire you to be your better self. So whether you are having trouble in a relationship or looking for inspiration to write that first novel, modern mantras will offer valuable insights to help you face some of life's many challenges. Read these mantras when you are up, down, or simply looking for a way forward.

www.

health

serenity

the present

hope

pain

conscience

guilt

letting go

peace

time

well-being

001>>>

Life is what you make it

002>>>

Stop trying to be a saint—it'll
go better for all of us

003>>>

*A second of time is a
second of mercy*

004>>>

Healthy body, healthy mind

005>>>

If I didn't write it down it never happened

006>>>

Take care of your body and it will take care of you

007>>> It is only when you are able to stand back from a situation that you can put it in perspective and see it for what it is.

It is not until you wake up from the dream that you own the wisdom of it

008>>> It's far better to be open and honest with both yourself and others and admit your hurts, than to bury the pain and suffer silently.

The hurts you keep inside leave the deepest scars

anon@youaretheauthor.com

009>>>

*Enjoy the little
things in life*

010>>>

Have a good cry
once in a while

011>>>

*There's no such thing
as a white lie*

012>>>

A guilty conscience
needs no accuser

013>>>

*You make your own
luck, good or bad*

014>>>

It's all in how
you look at things

015 >>> Everyone screws up, but it's important to learn from experience and move on. Try to turn a negative situation into a positive outcome.

Don't let the mistakes of your past be burdens that drag you down, but treasures you can carry with you

nicola_kamuk@yahoo.com

016>>> It's OK to come up against
obstacles. It is only by rising to a challenge that you
find out what you are capable of.

Don't be afraid of adversity—you may well be surprised by what you can do

anon@youaretheauthor.com

017>>>

Breathe deeply

018>>>

Always be here and now

019>>>

*If it's not leaking,
it's run out of oil*

020>>>

Bear and forebear

anon@youaretheauthor.com

021>>>

*To feel love, give love
to yourself and others*

022>>>

Character is worth
far more than money

023>>>

*A man who plans revenge
should best dig two graves*

anon@youaretheauthor.com

024>>> Don't settle for being an average
person—each of us is extraordinary.

Love deeply and
passionately…

…you might get hurt but it's the only way to live life completely

025>>> Being flexible and taking opportunities when they come your way isn't the same as being mercenary with your principles.

Open your arms to change, but don't let go of your values

suphetty76@hotmail.com

026>>> I try to remember that I am mostly afraid of the situations I am most ignorant of, so there's an easy solution—learn!

Fear always springs from ignorance

rog2llus@yahoo.com

027>>>

Know yourself

028>>>

Faith is the vision of the heart

029>>>

Memorize your favorite poem

030>>>

Beware the enemy within

031>>>

*Live every day as though
it were your last*

032>>>

Don't spend all you have
or sleep all you want

033>>>

*A diplomat is one who thinks
twice before saying nothing*

anon@youaretheauthor.com

034>>> We should all be free to do what most inspires us and feel good about living that way.

A man is successful if he gets up in the morning…

...goes to bed at night,
and in between does
what he wants to do

chailyngunners@hotmail.com

035>>> There are many things in life where the doing, the process of creating or developing something, is actually more important and more enjoyable than the end itself.

Enjoy the

process

036>>> If I feel any of these things, I know I have to stop and do something about it. I can't just struggle on expecting to operate properly and happily.

Hungry—Angry—
Lonely—Tired
means HALT

hamilton_harvey@yahoo.co.uk

037>>>

Ignorance breeds stupidity

038>>>

Listen to the silence

039>>>

Everything is possible

040>>>

The road to hell is paved
with good intentions

041>>>

A heart without love is like a violin without strings

042>>>

Think, then act, then feel

043>>>

Turn your face to the sun and the shadows fall behind you

044>>> We reach a point where it's
not enough to know something, we have to be willing
to step out in faith and start our real journey.

Faith begins
where reason ends

045>>> Very important for your well-being I think—walk the walk, don't just talk the talk.

Let your virtues speak for themselves

terri.racer@lycos.com

046>>>

Nothing great was ever
achieved without passion

047>>>

*Spend some time alone—
and get to know yourself*

048>>>

Don't live life from the outside in,
live from the inside out

049>>>

*What I want is
not always what I need*

050>>>

Once a year, go someplace
you've never been before

051>>>

*Guilt is the gift
that keeps on giving*

anon@youaretheauthor.com

052>>> Sometimes, not getting what you hoped for can turn out to be your good luck, because of the other opportunities that came your way, or because of the bad things you avoided.

Remember that not getting what you want is sometimes a stroke of good luck

053>>> Essentially, everything in life is temporary—including jobs, relationships, and problems that at the time seem insurmountable.

Kings and their realms pass away, but time goes on forever

seamus_t@dcemail.com

054>>> Whatever setbacks you encounter,
don't give up on your hopes and dreams.

Imagination is stronger than knowledge…

...dreams are more powerful than facts, and hope can triumph over experience

055>>> Don't undermine yourself—it's hard enough trying to be happy, even when your mind is on your side.

Negative thoughts are a waste of precious energy

056>>> I've learned that I can screw up the good times in my life if I'm not focused on the right things, being true to myself and enjoying without strings attached.

Every moment in time contains the seeds of happiness

anon@youaretheauthor.com

057>>> When I look back on some of
the things I missed, I am immeasurably thankful.

Mistakes are
proof that
you're trying

sam_o@hotmail.com

058>>> Congratulate yourself on what
you've done so far—it's no small achievement.

Look at how far you've come, not at how far you still have to go

mr.perfect@playful.com

059>>> Never waste time on wishful thinking or on unrealistic desires.

You can only choose from the options in front of you

060>>> It's easy enough to be
negative, it takes great strength to look on the bright
side.

Record only the
sunny hours and bring
the light into your life

ellyc89@hotmail.com

061 >>> Sometimes we need to own up
to the mistakes we have made in order to move on
from them.

A clear conscience is usually the sign of a bad memory

062>>> I guess I should keep my
expectations low then!

Good things come
when you least
expect them

063>>>

Happiness is an inside job

064>>>

Go with the flow

065>>>

Remember to put you first

066>>>

Every day is special

067>>>

It's alright letting yourself go,
as long as you can
get yourself back

068>>>

Let people feel the weight of who
you are, and let them deal with it

069>>> Don't get into a negative mind-set—
enjoy a happy, worry-free period while it lasts.

When a pessimist
has nothing to
worry about…

*...he worries about
why he has nothing
to worry about*

anon@youaretheauthor.com

070>>>

Never do card tricks for your poker buddies

071>>>

Be true to yourself

072>>>

Wonder is the beginning of wisdom

073>>>

*Don't cry because
it's over, smile
because it happened*

074>>>

Opportunities often
slip by unrecognized—
disguised as hard work

ambition

success

stress

workaholic

delegation

satisfaction

money

life balance

mistakes

colleagues

work

075>> You may have thought of the best idea in the world, but this is only half the task. Now you have to make your customers buy it. That is the tough part.

Success in business is often more about how you communicate than what you do

076>>> When things are not going well at work, remember that all problems present a challenge to be overcome.

Successful people don't talk about failure but use the words "setback" or "challenge"

anon@youaretheauthor.com

077>>>

Don't be offended by anything and never show fear

078>>>

Anyone who says money isn't important, hasn't got any

079>>>

A conclusion is the place where you got tired of thinking

080>>>

Stress is where you wake up screaming and realize you haven't even fallen asleep yet

081>>>

If you've got it, spend it

082>>>

Don't let work take over your life

anon@youaretheauthor.com

083>>>

The end crowns the work

084>>>

The first element of success is the will to succeed

085>>>

Speak softly and carry a big stick

086>>>

Be grateful for your work

087>>>

There is no such thing as a bad idea

088>>>

If a job's worth doing, it's because they pay you enough

089>>>

If you think nobody cares, try missing a couple of payments

anon@youaretheauthor.com

090>>> Sometimes it is better to stand back from a difficult situation and not take it too seriously. You are far more likely to find a solution this way than going into a panic.

If you can stay calm,

while all around

you is chaos…

…then you probably haven't completely understood the seriousness of the situation

mariollah@yahoo.com

091>>>

Always cover your ass

092>>>

Plagiarism saves time

093>>>

Success gets to be a habit

094>>>

A person who smiles in the
face of adversity
probably has a scapegoat

095>>>

*Go the extra mile—it makes
your boss look like an
incompetent slacker*

anon@youaretheauthor.com

096>>>

Never put off until tomorrow
what you can avoid altogether

097>>>

*When the going gets tough,
the tough take a coffee break*

098>>>

No one is listening
until you make a mistake

099>>>

Succeed in spite of management

100>>>

Are you hungry enough?

101>>>

Don't look at the clock

102>>>

Take a break between
completing tasks

anon@youaretheauthor.com

103>>> If I have the option, I sleep.

A snooze button
is a poor substitute
for no alarm clock at all

104>>> Life at the top can be damaging for all involved, far better to stay firmly on the terra-firma of average responsibility.

Eagles may soar, but weasels don't get sucked into jet engines

105>>>

*Don't burn your
bridges behind you*

106>>>

One of these days
is none of these days

107>>>

*If at first you don't succeed,
try management*

108>>>

I am proud with work,
I am proud without work

109>>>

Judge your success
by what you had to
give up in order to get it

110>>> Dont leave it for the temp to find out.

When you realize
you've made a mistake,
take immediate steps
to correct it

suphetty76@hotmail.com

111>>> Remember that at work, everyone can be replaced, so be flexible, otherwise you may never move on.

Don't think you're irreplaceable; if you can't be replaced, you can't be promoted

anon@youaretheauthor.com

1 1 2>>> Is your chairman obsessed with board meetings, motivational meetings, budget meetings? Maybe he should be worrying about the competition instead.

Rome did not create a great empire by having meetings…

…they did it by
killing all those
who opposed them

113>>> Everyone has an opinion, but you have to make the final decision.

The art of good leadership is to consider everyone's opinion but to make up your own mind

1 1 4>>> So don't bust a gut trying to improve your performance, just go for middle management like everyone else.

If at first you don't succeed, you're about average

115>>>

Whatever the boss says, goes

116>>>

The sooner you fall behind, the more time you'll have to catch up

117>>>

Work to live,
don't live to work

118>>>

Work smart, not hard

119>>>

What you are shows
in what you create

120>>>

One step leads to another

121>>>

You have to earn respect

122>>>

You get what you give

123>>>

Don't be caught flat-footed

124>>>

Not everyone has a
copy of my schedule

125>>>

*Everyone is equally
important in a company*

126>>>

Work, play, play play, play,
work, play, play play, play,
work, play, play play, play…

anon@youaretheauthor.com

127>>> It's foolish to drive yourself to an
early grave working too hard—remember to enjoy life as
you travel through it.

Go easy on yourself—

you can only

take so much

128>>> It is better to do a few things well than do many things badly and have to do them again.

It's a big thing to do a little thing well

anon@youaretheauthor.com

129>>>

*It is far easier to start
something than to finish it*

130>>>

A diamond is a piece of coal
that finished what it started

131>>>

*When in doubt, mumble;
when in trouble, delegate*

132>>>

If you want something
done right, do it yourself

133>>>

*Anything worth fighting for
is worth fighting dirty for*

134>>>

The absent are always
in the wrong

anon@youaretheauthor.com

135>>> And no one forgets to mail a bill, so stay several checks ahead at all times even still, good luck…

Bills travel through the mail at twice the speed of checks

136>>> The important thing is not that
a million things get done, but that the one important
thing is done with excellence.

Quality,
not quantity

love

friendship

priorities

arguments

be yourself

honesty

passion

soul mates

early days

long term

relationships

137>>>

One is enough

138>>>

When I stop looking,
I find what I need

139>>>

Think twice before you speak

140>>>

I am still an individual
when I am with someone

141>>>

Always is a long time

142>>>

All experience is
education for the soul

anon@youaretheauthor.com

143>>> Intransigence and lack of understanding usually lead to confrontational situations. Try to see the other person's point of view.

Anyone who doesn't think there are two sides to an argument is probably in one

anon@youaretheauthor.com

144>>> I say this to myself when I find I'm getting annoyed with someone for no obvious reason. Sometimes, I can see something of myself in their behavior...

Mirror, mirror,
on the wall...

holy_jo@witty.com

145>>> Communication between the sexes must be possible, and it is. So don't get so pessimistic about it all, and make more effort to be understanding.

Men are from earth, women are from earth, deal with it

146>>> So remember more
anniversaries than you think could possibly matter.

It's the little things
that count

anon@youaretheauthor.com

147>>> It can be done, in the workplace, at home, with relationships. By using problems as opportunities to overcome and grow, we make situations work for us.

Turn negatives into positives

148>>> Don't make fixed judgments about people before you get a chance to know them properly. They may surprise you.

Don't be too quick to judge

anon@youaretheauthor.com

149>>>

*Kindness is contagious
and so is anger*

150>>>

I am free to go, so I stay

151>>>

*Better to ask the way
than go astray*

152>>>

People are a mass
of inconsistencies

153>>>

*Everybody deserves
to be loved*

154>>>

A fight is a great way
to clear the air

anon@youaretheauthor.com

155>>> Be as generous in dealing with the faults of others as you would like them to be generous toward you—it usually pays dividends.

Deal with the faults of others as gently as you would your own

156>>> People will say all kinds of things in the first flush of a relationship, but often the most passionate beginnings quickly burn out. Wait until things are more settled to understand the true nature of a relationship.

Never believe anything your lover says in the first month of a relationship

157>>> Better the hollow shell of insincerity and suspicion than no relationship at all?

The key to any relationship is sincerity—once you can fake that, the rest is easy

158>>> There are many issues in a loving relationship that should be handled with delicacy and compassion. Don't ride roughshod over your partner's feelings.

Travel as light as possible over heavy ground

anon@youaretheauthor.com

159>>>

*There is a big gap
between advice and help*

160>>>

If sex is all you want,
then sex is all you'll get

161>>>

*Your time is the greatest gift
you can give to someone*

162>>>

I think—therefore I'm single

163>>>

Love will find a way

164>>>

Variety is the spice of life

165>>>

People need people

166>>> Don't open that Pandora's box, it just
spreads hurt and distrust.

In disagreements
with loved ones…

...deal with the current situation—don't bring up the past

167>>> Relationships cannot be constructed and forced to work—just let things develop naturally.

Let your friends call you for a change

168>>> The quickest way to ruin a relationship is to try to control or force the other person to live up to your expectations.

You can't build a relationship with a hammer

ssedric@email.com

169>>>

You can't please everyone

170>>>

A friend is easier
lost than found

171>>>

Friends may come and go,
but enemies accumulate

172>>>

Remember that great love
and great achievements
involve great risk

173>>>

*The most important relationship
in my life is the one with myself*

174>>>

A person who is nice to you,
but rude to the waiter,
is not a nice person

anon@youaretheauthor.com

175>>> Be open to the possibility of
forming friendships, even when you least expect to.

Strangers are just

friends waiting

to happen

176>>> Pride can easily blow small matters out of all proportion. Get some perspective and remember what's important.

Don't let a little dispute injure a great friendship

177>>>

One plus one, makes one

178>>>

Read between the lines

179>>>

My friends are precious

180>>>

I can learn from others

181>>>

*The best cure for a
short temper is a long walk*

182>>>

True wealth is
having good friends

183>>>

*You don't know what
you've got till it's gone*

anon@youaretheauthor.com

home

children

parents

love

fights

growing up

patience

life

lessons

family unit

family

184>>>

Family first

185>>>

*Our house is clean
enough to be healthy and
dirty enough to be happy*

186>>>

Your family is your rock

187>>>

Your family is there to help you
appreciate your friends

188>>>

If you do housework badly
enough, you'll never be asked
to do it again

189>>>

Housework done
properly can kill you

anon@youaretheauthor.com

190>>> Men always make a big deal about the
little work they do around the home.

A husband is someone
who takes out the trash…

...and gives the impression that he just cleaned the whole house

191>>> This is one my nephew told
me (he's only 3).

What would the cow say
to the zebra if they
met on the high street?
You're a zebra, you are

192>>> I try to think of the things I missed in my home, and make sure they are there for my kids.

A loving atmosphere is so important—do all you can to create a tranquil, harmonious home

brandon_top@musician.org

193>>>

*My parents loved me as
much as they could*

194>>>

All things grow with love

195>>>

*No one is easy to
live with all of the time*

196>>>

My family is from Mars

197>>>

Family is life

198>>>

Share your knowledge with
your children—it's one way to
achieve immortality

199>>>

*All families are mad
in their own way*

anon@youaretheauthor.com

200>>> If you've got kids, make sure
they know what it is that they do well, and help bring
out these skills.

No one is good at everything, but everyone is good at something

201>>> I think this is a paraphrase of a famous quote, but it sums up the way I feel about my family. I know I can go home and find my wife and two sons there. They give me the courage and the determination to carry on.

Give me a solid base and I can move the world

anon@youaretheauthor.com

202>>>

Kids in the back seat cause accidents; accidents in the back seat cause kids

203>>>

Love is unconditional

204>>>

I do not have to accept my inheritance

205>>>

Call your mom

206>>>

Roses grow out of manure

207>>>

Children change everything

208>>>

Don't judge people
by their relatives

209>>> Never, ever say anything sensitive in your own house.

Walls have ears

hou_wal@dcemail.com

210>>> And don't punish them for it, they only get one chance.

Let kids be kids

anon@youaretheauthor.com

211>>> So remember her birthday!

God could not be everywhere— therefore he made mothers

anon@youaretheauthor.com

212>>> Weren't you? So don't get
angry if accidents result, it's all in innocence.

Kids are naturally

curious

213>>> I always found this true in my
childhood, and it hasn't changed since.

When mother ain't happy,
ain't nobody happy

www.

problems

art

expression

spirituality

solutions

success

willpower

experience

brainstorms

ideas

creativity

214>>>

*We all possess the power to
manifest every desire we have*

215>>>

Do it now—
tomorrow never comes

216>>>

*Creativity is like a muscle—
it gets bigger and stronger
with use*

217>>>

Creativity is the expression
of the inexpressible

218>>>

*No one can ever understand
anything someone else says*

219>>>

I can't distil my experience
into a few words

220>>> Sometimes, the simplest answer is
not a single one. When presented with a complex question,
break it down and the answer(s) will swiftly follow!

Q) What can you sit on, sleep in, and brush your teeth with?

A) A chair, a bed, and a toothbrush

221>>>

*Things often happen when
you least expect them*

222>>>

If it ain't broke, don't fix it

223>>>

*There's no such thing
as a noncreative person*

224>>>

To create is to make
the world again

225>>>

*Use your whole
being to create*

226>>> Sometimes I already have the thing I
need to solve a problem, without going to great lengths.

See what is under
your nose, first

227>>> In school I always hated it when teachers gave us projects and told us to be creative. These were my worst slumps in creativity, because I was trying to be creative.

To be creative,
be yourself

lombok@beliefnet.com

228>>>

Creativity is believing in God

229>>>

Everything around you was created

230>>>

We live in a creative universe

231>>>

Trying isn't doing

232>>>

Two brains are better than one

233>>>

Creativity is the lens of truth

234>>> It's always when you are
under pressure of deadlines or finances to come up
with a creative solution that you can't.

*Creativity comes
when you least expect it*

235>>> It's all about having good
ideas, innovative ideas. This is what makes the
world go around.

Great ideas are the
fuel of progress

236>>> I use this mantra to focus me when I have to be creative in my work. While I have to follow the client's brief, I still try to put a bit of myself into the work. This helps me to do my best, even with a very small and straightforward project.

What you are shows in what you create

237>>> I want everything that I make
to be complete and whole and to have its own being
and existence, separate from me, its maker.

Like life,
art involves the
meeting of mind,
body, and spirit

anon@youaretheauthor.com

238>>>

*Creativity is me
talking to myself*

239>>>

We are made from stardust

240>>>

*Creativity is recycling—create
from what is around you*

241>>>

There are no rules for creativity

242>>>

If I can't laugh, I can't create

anon@youaretheauthor.com

wisdom

thought

learning

health

focus

identity

confidence

challenges

reading

achieving

intelligence

243>>> All through school, I was told that I was stupid. I have since realized that I am intelligent, just not in the way that my teachers wanted me to be. As soon as I understood this, I was able to use my intelligence and have confidence in my abilities.

I will allow myself to use my natural intelligence

fiona_prof@teacher.com

244>>> Finding answers is not the answer—life is a process, a journey of discovery, and it is the process itself that gives life meaning.

*What's the point
of living if you already
know the meaning of life*

anon@youaretheauthor.com

245>>>

I don't have to attend every
argument I'm invited to

246>>>

Grasp all, lose all

247>>>

Easy come easy go—
but the difficult things
will stay forever

248>>>

Live and learn

249>>>

Intelligence is not the
same as wisdom

250>>>

Feed your brain

251>>> Remember that even a minority of one can be right; don't doubt yourself or your intelligence.

Sometimes the majority

only means that all

the fools are

on the same side

252>>> The quality of my decisions
has a lot to do with my state of my mind at the time.

Clear head,
clear choices

253>>>

Never believe generalizations

254>>>

True wisdom is to live
in the present, plan for the
future, and profit from the past

255>>>

Worrying never changed anything

256>>>

Don't think too much

257>>>

True intelligence is knowing how stupid you are

258>>>

Whoever wins the war gets to write the history

259>>>

Empty your mind and the right answer will come

anon@youaretheauthor.com

260>>> Your views will change so
much over time, it's best to be aware.

Keep an open mind

261 >>> It's not easy to look the truth straight in the face, but once you have, you feel released and unburdened.

The truth will set you free, but first it will piss you off

262>>> Good books should challenge
you to think for yourself.

*The book to read is not
the one which thinks
for you, but the one
which makes you think*

anon@youaretheauthor.com

263>>> There is always room for this
one in my life.

Read more books
and watch less TV

264>>>

You can't fit a square peg in a round hole

265>>>

Trust in God but lock your car

266>>>

If you can smile when things go wrong, you have someone in mind to blame

267>>>

A library is a hospital for the mind

268>>>

*Don't finish a book
just because you started it*

269>>>

Stop learning and you might as well stop breathing

270>>> Beware of anyone listening too intently
to what you have to say...

You have the right to

remain silent...

*...anything you say
will be misquoted,
then used against you*

271>>>

Slow and steady
wins the race

272>>>

*Wisdom is knowing
the right questions*

273>>>

Clever people are usually
the craziest people I know

274>>>

Be still

275>>>

To think is to discover
freedom within

276>>>

I'm not just intelligent

277>>>

I can't think
myself happy

www.

change

negativity

motivation

healing

perspective

courage

facing life

choices

friends

self-belief

depression

278>>>

Nothing lasts forever

279>>>

Never say die

280>>>

My natural state is happy

281>>>

Time heals all wounds

282>>>

*Hard times are inevitable,
but misery is optional*

283>>>

This will pass

anon@youaretheauthor.com

284>>> OK, the ending is a bit silly, but it is always worth putting yourself in another person's position to truly understand them.

Before you criticize someone, you should walk a mile in their shoes…

...that way you're a mile away from them and you have their shoes

285>>> In the long run I think I've found that even the worst things can work out for the best—most of the time.

Things happen
for the best

286>>> Sometimes I just have to remember this and it gets me motivated again.

Snap out of it, and pull yourself together

287>>>   Self-belief is all that really
matters—you can do it if you want to.

Whether you think you can, or you think you can't, you'll be right both ways

288>>> I get depressed when I look at
things in a negative way.

Cheer up! Remember, the less you have, the more there is to get

anon@youaretheauthor.com

289>>>

Take it one day
at a time

290>>>

*Don't treat the symptom,
instead find the cause*

291>>>

I do my best

292>>>

*There's no way
down from the bottom*

293>>>

Give time time

294>>> For me, depression is usually a
problem with my perspective on things. Saying this helps
me see things at their proper scale.

It's not the end
of the world

295>>> This comes from seeing that most of
my heartache stems from my own stubbornness, and that it
heals itself ultimately by necessity.

When the pain of
remaining the same
exceeds the pain of
change, you will change

ali.patt@lycos.com

296>>>

*Your friends love you
for who you are*

297>>>

Everyone has problems

298>>>

*Live and learn,
learn to live*

299>>>

If nothing changes,
nothing changes

300>>>

*I've given up
being miserable—it's
too much hassle*

www.

clarity

resolve

perspective

ambition

time

judgment

belief

guidance

learning

mistakes

life in focus

301>>>

Distance clarifies everything

302>>>

It is far more impressive when others discover your good qualities without your help

303>>>

Some days you are the bug, some days you are the windshield

304>>>

Don't give up hoping

305>>>

Following the path of least resistance is what makes rivers and men crooked

306>>>

Find out what you
don't do well, then don't do it

307>>> Life is a learning process, and you can never be right all the time.

Good judgment comes from bad experiences…

...and a lot of those are caused by bad judgment

anon@youaretheauthor.com

308>>>

The secret of happiness
is not to expect

309>>>

*Be good; and if you can't
be good, be careful*

310>>>

You can't hug a child
with nuclear arms

311>>>

*The biggest sin of all
is to waste time*

312>>>

Garbage in, garbage out

313>>>

*Failure is the path
of least persistence*

anon@youaretheauthor.com

314>>> Remembering this saves me much trouble, what a relief that nobody's perfect.

What a joy it is to be an imperfect human

315>>> Unless you're learning a
language. Otherwise, try to listen a bit more.

*Generally speaking,
you aren't learning
much when your
mouth is moving*

mike_pritch20@yahoo.co.uk

316>>>

Flexible people don't
get bent out of shape

317>>>

*Everybody's your brother
until the rent is due*

318>>>

If you can't beat 'em,
try beating 'em again

319>>>

Everything in moderation—
unless it's really good

320>>>

God gave me my life,
it belongs to Him

321>>>

No matter what happens,
somebody will find a way to
take it too seriously

322>>> Most things don't matter that
much in the long term, so chill out a bit!

Nothing is ever as good
or as bad as it may seem

323>>> I can't drink my problems away, only deal with them in sobriety.

Solutions are not found at the bottom of bottles

324>>> Sometimes there are good reasons not to blindly rush in, but let others lead the way instead.

The early bird gets the worm, but the second mouse gets the cheese

325>>> There are many lessons to
learn from the Zen of traffic.

*The other line always
moves faster until
you join it*

anon@youaretheauthor.com

326>>>

Don't confuse logic with life

327>>>

Everyone has a message for us

328>>>

Do what is right, come what may

329>>>

God wants the best for me

330>>>

I believe the only time the world
beats a path to my door is when
I'm in the bathroom

331>>>

*Appearances aren't
necessarily deceptive*

332>>>

When I look at nature,
I know that God is great

333>>> I don't always learn from my mistakes,
but I try not to let this get me down!

*Experience is a
wonderful thing…*

...it enables you to recognize a mistake when you make it again

anon@youaretheauthor.com

My idea of housework is to sweep a room with a glance

335>>> Never be afraid to go for plan "b"—or to reevaluate yourself.

Even the best laid plans go awry

anon@youaretheauthor.com

336>>>

Keep it real

337>>>

I am myself and my circumstances

338>>>

Focus on now

339>>>

A salmon in the can is worth six in the sea

anon@youaretheauthor.com

340>>>

Everybody makes mistakes

341>>>

If you must choose between evils, pick the one you've never tried before

342>>> Which is better for all us
stupid people.

If you always tell
the truth, you don't have
to remember anything

343>>> It's pretty straight forward. If
it doesn't make sense to you, think about it more.

*Your mind is your
greatest ally and your
greatest enemy*

renegade13@beliefnet.com

344>>>

Looks can be deceiving

345>>>

*The only real test
in life is to conquer your fears*

346>>>

Can't see the forest for the trees

347>>>

*Don't bite the hand
that feeds you*

348>>>

Everything comes
to those who wait

349>>>

*It is not important what you
believe, only that you believe*

350>>>

You can live in a car
but you can't drive a house

anon@youaretheauthor.com

351 >>> I try not to be quick to judge the value or benefit of a gift or a bit of luck, this devalues the source, and my gratitude.

Don't look a gift horse in the mouth

352>>> I find the kitchen a far more
exciting venue than before in either case.

Approach love and cooking with reckless abandon

anon@youaretheauthor.com

353>>> Try to be aware of your mood changing and your patience slipping—it could save you from saying something you regret.

Patience is never more important…

...than when you are on the verge of losing it

354>>> If you believe this, you'll live
a very sad and unfulfilled existence.

He who dies with
the most toys wins

355>>> Being nice doesn't mean drawing the short straw all the time. Good actions come back to bless me.

It pays to be nice

anon@youaretheauthor.com

356>>>

Go beyond your comfort zone

357>>>

*More than enough
is too much*

358>>>

Make do with what you have

359>>>

*Don't expect things to
go right the first time*

360>>>

Life is one big experiment

361>>>

You have to take the bitter with the sweet

362>>>

It takes one to know one

anon@youaretheauthor.com

363>>> Whether you believe in a higher power or not, there seems to be a form of divine justice out there.

God pays debts

without money

364>>> Make sure it's not you—
laugh first

He who laughs last
thinks slowest

365>>>

Take life as it comes

366>>>

Stop and smell the roses

367>>>

There must be an easier way

368>>>

Get some perspective

369>>>

*Never spend your money
before you have it*

370>>>

Truth fears no questions

371>>>

*Make the most of
every situation*

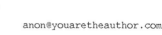

anon@youaretheauthor.com

372>>> There are going to be times
when you need to be firm, and a hard word now can
stop a bigger problem later.

Hard words break
no bones

373>>> We all have expectations of
life, just don't expect them to be met.

Life—it's nothing like
the brochure

anon@youaretheauthor.com

374>>>

Life is for living

375>>>

Time and tide wait for no man

376>>>

There's a time and a place
for everything

377>>>

What you cannot avoid, welcome

378>>>

Lead me not into temptation
(I can find the way myself)

379>>>

*Over 150,000 people
die every day*

380>>>

The end of one thing is merely
the beginning of another

381 >>> It certainly makes life easier.

Money can't buy you happiness…

…*but it can
make unhappiness
more comfortable*

index

If you feel inspired by any of the mantras in this book,
why not log on to *www.youaretheauthor.com*? Specially
created to provide an outlet for your experience and creativity,
the site is your chance to give a world-wide audience the
benefit of your wisdom—and perhaps get your words
published in the next *www.youaretheauthor.com* book.